Practising th

with
Brother Lawrence

by
Jennifer Moorcroft

*All booklets are published thanks to the
generous support of the members of the
Catholic Truth Society*

CATHOLIC TRUTH SOCIETY
PUBLISHERS TO THE HOLY SEE

2

Contents

A message that speaks today

When there is turmoil in the Church and the world, as there often is, then God raises up people of exceptional holiness to act as beacons for the way ahead. His usual choice is, in the words of Saint Paul,[1] one who is foolish in the eyes of the world, of no account, one not wise by worldly standards. So it was that in the 17th Century he raised up a humble Carmelite lay brother, one who was, in his own words, 'a clumsy awkward fellow', to be a light in the turmoil that gripped the Europe of his day.

His life and times

Nicolas Herman was born of a poor family in the Lorraine region of France, and entered the Carmelites when he was 28 years of age, taking the name of Lawrence of the Resurrection, dying in 1691, at the age of 77. Employed first in the kitchen and then in making sandals for the community, his holiness and the simplicity of his message gradually spread out to some of the most influential people of his time, and far beyond his homeland of France.

There were three main areas of conflict to which his simple message, that of the practice of the presence of God, spoke. He lived in the aftermath of the Protestant

Revolution, with Catholic and Protestants at war with each other. The Catholic Faith was coming under attack, and in response God raised up many outstanding saints who led the process of reform in the Counter-Reformation, such saints as Francis de Sales, Teresa of Avila, Ignatius Loyola, Philip Neri, to name just a few. In France, the desire for renewal, above all the search for prayer and for holiness, was especially strong among such people as Bérulle, François Fénélon, Barbe Acarie, Bossuet, but one of the most influential of these people, outstanding in his holiness, was our lowly Carmelite lay brother, Lawrence of the Resurrection.

Because, after his death, his writings were referred to in the quietist controversy, they were not well known in his own country but achieved amazing success in other countries, where both Protestants and Catholics found in him a sure and endearing guide in the spiritual life. Where wars failed to unite, a simple spirituality of the practice of the presence of God did. The writings of Brother Lawrence found such diverse admirers as John Wesley, the founder of Methodism, Thomas Kelly, a Quaker, and Aldous Huxley the atheist.

Because of the conflict between Catholics and Protestants, many European countries were drawn into the Thirty Years War – in which Brother Lawrence himself participated. Many of these countries were mainly lost to the Catholic Church, but when the Church is under attack God never abandons it. He provides the best weapon, not the arms of warfare, but the holiness and example of her children. Lawrence had borne arms, but he achieved far more by the message that was entrusted to him.

His legacy

Can his message speak to us today? I believe it can, for in so many ways his teaching has a special relevance to our times. Many only experience God as absent and find it difficult to see God present, both in the world and within themselves. Lawrence, too, experienced this 'absence' for some ten long years, feeling himself outside the mercy of God, but he never abandoned his search or allowed his love to grow dim. In this search, he found God both within and everywhere.

Many are hungering for silence and for the ability to find small spaces within a busy day to find themselves and to find God. Lawrence shows us the way; he shows us how to make small pockets of 'awareness' in the most unconducive of situations, because the busy Carmelite kitchen was no less pressured, noisy with the clash of pans, and tiring, than many a workplace today!

When the idea that we can speak to God and that God speaks to us is often greeted with derision and implications of delusion in the secular world, Lawrence affirms that we can indeed speak to God; indeed, that it is an integral part of our human existence. He assures us that God likewise, and pre-eminently, speaks to us. He comes to us as a friend. Teresa of Avila, when asked why she no longer had ecstasies towards the end of her life, responded simply, 'we understand each other'. Pope Benedict XVI said, 'I always pray first and foremost to our Lord, with whom I am united simply by old acquaintance, so to speak.'

Then the Pope added, 'But I also invoke the saints. I am friends with Augustine, with Bonaventure, with Thomas Aquinas.'[2] In his writings, Lawrence shows us the simplicity of this dialogue and how to enter into it. And when we meet him in the testimonies of those who knew him, perhaps we, too, like the Pope, will find in him a friend for ourselves, living no less vividly now than three hundred years ago. As his friend and publisher, Joseph de Beaufort, said, when you met him you felt as if you had met a true friend.

The attraction to God's love

Brother Lawrence was born Nicolas Herman in Hériménil, a small village near Luneville in Lorraine, a region of eastern France. The parish church in which the birth records were kept was set fire to during the Thirty Years War and the records destroyed, and for some time the date of his birth was uncertain. However, from the records kept by the Carmelites it has now been established that he was born in 1614. He seems to have been an only child, but he was surrounded by a village network of close family relations. His parents, Dominic and Louise, were poor but devout, and he was brought up in an atmosphere of Christian faith and sturdy good sense.

In later life he was sometimes dismissed as simple-minded, ignorant and uneducated, none of which was true, but it was probably a testament to his humility that he was content to be thought so. In fact, he was well-read according to the standards of the time. The parish priest gave him lessons, supplemented by lessons in his faith at home. It is a measure of the esteem in which he held his parish priest that he took the name of Lawrence when he entered religious life; it was also the name of the village's patron saint. The villagers were unanimous in testifying that he was responsible, dependable and reliable. He would also prove himself highly intelligent, level-headed and a sure spiritual guide himself in later life.

Army life

Because of his family's poverty, Nicolas enlisted in the army at an early age, which ensured that he would have enough food to eat and a small stipend. Much later, he wrote a letter concerning a young man in the army, which may reflect his own experience, because even then he had a love of God:

> May he think of him [God] as much as possible, especially in times of greatest danger. A brief lifting up of the heart is enough. A brief remembrance of God, an act of inner adoration - even though on the run with sword in hand – these prayers, short as they may be, are pleasing to God and, far from causing those engaged in battle to lose courage in the most dangerous circumstances, fortify them... It is very appropriate and necessary for a soldier who is always exposed to threats to his life and often to his salvation.[3]

However, he later spoke of the sins of his youth, and the war was bloody and brutal. Was he drawn, despite his reluctance, into the looting and violence that was part of soldiering? It is possible that the evil that he saw all around him made him feel complicit in that evil.

Close to death

The Thirty Years War had started in 1618 and Nicolas joined the army of Lorraine, which was opposing the invasion of the German troops under Charles V, Duke of Lorraine, who was trying to recapture the duchies and states which he had lost. At one point Nicolas was captured by some German soldiers who were convinced that he was a spy and threatened to hang him. Nicolas responded that he had a clear conscience and furthermore, was not afraid to die. Impressed by his evident uprightness of character and transparent honesty, he was released unharmed.

He rejoined the Lorraine army and then the Swedes joined the conflict and invaded Lorraine. In 1635 their army laid siege to the small village of Rambervilliers. It was defended by seven hundred men, and when Charles V breeched the walls he forced the defendants to surrender on 10 August, the Feast of Saint Lawrence. Nicolas was wounded and was sent back to his own village nearby to recuperate. The sciatic nerve in his leg had nearly been severed, and he was left permanently lamed and in chronic pain, with complications that often led to fevers and infection. His military career was over.

Conversion experience

During his period in the army, when he was eighteen
years of age, he had had a profound experience that
changed him spiritually and which he called his
conversion. It was during the winter, and he saw a tree
stripped of its leaves and fruit, to all appearances
lifeless. Nicolas was then made vividly aware that he,
too, seemingly dead like the tree, was nevertheless
assured of a springtime of resurrection. The incident
was almost commonplace, but for Nicolas, it 'lifted him
up immediately to God, and inspired him with so
sublime an awareness that this impression was still as
strong and intense in his soul forty years later'.[4]

He did not allow this experience to lie fallow or
remain simply a vivid memory; it prompted him to
begin to search for God more deeply in prayer and to
find out what path God wanted him to follow.

Drawn to the Carmelites

When he was recovered enough he left home, drawn to
give himself totally to God, but without knowing how to
do so and what God wanted of him. He was still
troubled in mind, sick of the worldliness and the casual
violence of the war, where the whole region had been
devastated by the war, and plague and famine.

A certain prosperous gentleman nearby, who wanted to live more closely evangelical poverty, had retired to a hermitage and Nicolas joined him there. It was not a success. The life of a hermit needs a person who is advanced in the spiritual life, and Nicholas realised that such a life was not for him and that at this stage of his life he needed expert guidance.

> Our new solitary realized this clearly [that the eremitical life was not for beginners] as he saw joy, sadness, peace, disturbance, fervour, distraction, trust and despondency reign one after the other in his heart, and he therefore began to doubt the validity of his way.[5]

He realised that he needed the support of a community that would give a firm foundation to his desire for progress in the spiritual life. A short while earlier, in 1633, an uncle of his, his mother's brother, John Majeur, had entered the Carmelite Priory in Paris, and perhaps this encouraged Nicolas to make his way to Paris, where his uncle could advise him and counsel him as to his way ahead. Although he was drawn to the Carmelite way of life, for the present he did not follow his uncle into the Paris priory. Instead, he was taken on as a footman in the house of M. de Fieubet, treasurer of the Exchequer as well as a King's Councillor and

Chancellor to the Queen. It was not an easy time, and Nicolas himself described himself as an awkward, clumsy fellow who broke things. He did not consider that his disabilities contributed to his awkwardness, but it humiliated him and he felt that he had to make amends.

It was in 1640, now convinced that God really did want him to follow the religious life, despite his profound sense of his own unworthiness, that he entered the Carmelites as a lay brother. He said that he entered religion in order to atone for his past mistakes and clumsiness, but he found also a depth of union with God and a joy and contentment that he would never have believed possible.

First steps in Carmel

The Carmelite Priory in Paris on the Rue de Vaurigard was only the second house of Discalced Carmelites of friars, after Avignon, to be established in France, although eight monasteries of the nuns had already arrived there. In 1613, the Queen Mother, Marie de Medicis had laid the first stone. The new foundation was slow to grow, and there were few novices when Nicolas entered.

Training

He spent two months in his secular clothes before receiving the habit and entering into the two year period of the novitiate. He shared this training with the brothers who would become priests of the Order, but with the additional instruction suited to his vocation as a lay brother. Among the books they studied were the works of Saint John of the Cross and Saint Teresa of Avila. Fr. Louis of Saint Teresa, the Prior, instructed Fr. Julien of the Cross, the Novice Master, to read the two authors to his novices alternately for three months at a time. It was Saint John of the Cross who had the most influence on him.

Another profound influence on Brother Lawrence was the text book of Venerable John of Jesus and Mary, also one of the staple books of the Novitiate, and who, perhaps more than any other, influenced Lawrence to stop his occupations every so often to say a short prayer of adoration.

Brother Lawrence asserted that the Lord had tricked him, because he had entered religious life in order to be severely reprimanded for his previous sins, but had instead found only satisfaction. Nevertheless, his Novice Master did treat him with greater severity than the other novices, because he already recognised that Lawrence had sterling qualities and would grow in virtue through such testing. Two years later he made his Profession on 14 August 1642, at the age of 28.

Work in the kitchen

For the first fifteen years after his Profession Brother Lawrence was assigned to work in the kitchen. There seemed to be no complaints about broken dishes here, so the poorer, heavier dishes of the Carmelites seemed easier for him to handle than the plate of the gentry. The work was uncongenial to him, noisy, with the clashing of pots and pans, and heavy work which was doubly difficult for him with his lameness, with the demands for his service from all quarters and the monotony of the work. The Paris Carmel became a training centre for new entrants, and at some points housed up to a hundred friars, so it was hard work to provide for such a large number. Between 1674 and1676 an extra floor was added to the monastery to cater for the influx of recruits. Brother Lawrence would undoubtedly have been encouraged by the fact that Saint Teresa had also taken her turn at working in the kitchen and that she found it difficult to remain recollected. 'Teresa', the Lord replied to her complaint about this, 'you are not in heaven yet.' Still, Teresa also affirmed that she found God among the pots and pans, and so did Lawrence.

Prayer in the kitchen

Lawrence was determined, despite his initial aversion to working in the kitchen, that he would make it the vehicle of his prayer and an expression of his love for God. Before he started his work in the kitchen he would think about what his work involved, and then how he would carry out each task, doing everything for the love of God, and asking God for the grace to do everything well. He described the way in which he trained himself:

> We must perform all our actions carefully and deliberately, not impulsively or hurriedly, for such would characterise a distracted mind. We must work gently and lovingly with God, asking him to accept our work, and by this continual attention to God we will crush the head of the devil and force the weapons from his hands.[6]

Consequently, the brothers noticed that, however busy and hurried the work was he never lost his recollected calm, neither over hasty nor loitering, but 'with an even, uninterrupted composure and tranquillity of spirit'. 'His very countenance was edifying; such a sweet and calm devotion appearing in it as could not but affect those who saw him.'

Love of God is expressed in love of our neighbour, and as cook Lawrence had opportunity to do this. He could supply the needs of the poor who came to the kitchen door, and catering for his brothers in the monastery; 'he took pleasure in pleasing them as if they were angels'.[7]

His prior, Louis de Sainte-Thérèse, defined Lawrence's vocation as one of work and prayer, and this was what he pursued. Because the work of the lay brothers meant that they were not often free to take part in community prayer, they said their vocal prayers and took their times of meditation when they could. When his work in the kitchen finished, Lawrence would immediately go to a small oratory next to the kitchen and pray there. This was an oratory recommended by Venerable John of Jesus and Mary, and, mindful of the incident in the life of Teresa of Avila, who received her conversion before a painting of Christ at the pillar, contained one also. He would often spend the nights in prayer before the Blessed Sacrament. Nevertheless, prayer was far from easy for him.

Time of trial

For the first ten years of his Carmelite life he went through a testing time of trial; prayer was difficult, and even when he received graces in prayer he dismissed them as untrue because he considered that he did not deserve them. What he saw as the sins of his previous life were so overwhelming to him that his mind and soul were in torment. He wrote later to his spiritual director that:

> the apprehension that I did not belong to God as I wished, my past sins always before my eyes, and the lavish graces God gave me, were the sum and substance of all my woes. During this period I fell often, but I got back up just as quickly. It seemed to me that all creatures, reason, and God himself were against me, and that faith alone was on my side.[8]

In his distress, he would often go to that little oratory next to the kitchen, and before the painting of Our Lord at the pillar, 'his heart distraught, and completely bathed in his tears, he poured out his feelings before his God and begged him not to let him perish, because he had placed all his trust in him and intended only to please him'.[9]

Sense of unworthiness

Part of this agony was that on the one hand he was overwhelmed by the brightness of the divine light of God the closer he moved towards God, while at the same time he was paralysed by the thought of his own wretchedness. Yet he felt himself far from the vision of God, which was an additional torment for him.[10]

For the last four years of this period he was tormented by the conviction that he was damned. Nevertheless, the love of God that had entered into him at the time of his 'conversion' sustained him, as he reasoned that:

> I entered religious life solely for the love of God, and have tried to act for him alone. Whether I be damned or saved, I always want to act purely for his love; at least I can say this that, until I die, I will do whatever I can to love him.[11]

He wanted to give God 'all for all', regardless of how he felt.

Prayer of simplicity

During his novitiate he had spent his times of prayer in thinking of God more by devout sentiments than by reasoning and elaborate meditations. In the early years of his religious life he read many books to help him, and prayed with the help of various devotions, methods of prayer and set prayers, but none of them really suited him. His time of prayer was often spent in rejecting wandering thoughts and then falling back into them.

Gradually he developed a method of prayer that he termed 'the practice of the presence of God'. He started and ended his work each day in the kitchen with a prayer, and during his work did it as if he was doing it for God alone; the least little task, even picking up a straw or flipping an omelette, was done for the love of God. He also tried to keep up a continual conversation with God during his work, reminding himself of his presence and gently turning back to him when his thoughts strayed, given the necessary need for the concentration required for his work.

At first, he found this difficult but it gradually became habitual. Further, he began to realise that this 'practice of the presence of God' was flowing over into his times of prayer and that he no longer needed books or devotional practices and set prayers, apart from the '*Paters Nosters*' and '*Ave Marias*' that he recited as a lay brother.

Act of abandonment

This time of testing came to an end when Lawrence was content to remain in this condition for the rest of his life, a state which he said did not at all lessen the trust he had in God, but which served only to increase his faith. As soon as he had made this act of abandonment 'I found myself changed all at once; and my soul, which till this time was in trouble, felt a profound inward peace as if it were in her centre and place of rest'.[12] He had broken through to a new and permanent state in his spiritual life.

He was speaking from his own experience when, years later, he wrote to a sister of the Blessed Sacrament, an Order that had a convent next door to the monastery:

> I know that to reach this state, the first steps are very difficult, and that we must act purely in faith. Furthermore, we know we can do anything with God's grace, and that he never refuses it to those who earnestly ask for it. Knock at his door, keep knocking, and I tell you that he will open to you in his time if you do not give up, and that he will give you, all at once, what he held off giving for years.[13]

It is not as if he no longer thought of his sins, his faults and failings, because he continued to see them only too clearly, calling himself the most miserable of all human beings, but now he no longer saw them in the light of God's condemnation but in the true light of God's merciful love. He was established in an unshakeable peace that never deserted him.

Perhaps he knew the poem 'Teresa's Bookmark', as it is affectionately known, and now understood how profoundly true it was:

Let nothing trouble you,
Let nothing afright you,
All is fleeting,
God alone is unchanging.
Patience
Everything obtains.
Who possesses God
Nothing wants.
God alone suffices.

Practising the presence of God

Having found such benefit in this way of prayer for himself, Lawrence was eager to share it with others, and in his letters, writings and conversations gave invaluable guidance as to how to practice it. However, it is not to be thought that this practice was new in the Church since it lies at the very heart of Judeo-Christian spirituality. Every Christian is called to live in the presence of God, but sometimes an aspect of the spiritual life becomes overlooked and God then raises up an exceptional person to remind us of that perhaps forgotten aspect, or to show it forth in a new and more emphatic way.

Immersed in the Carmelite tradition

Brother Lawrence would have found ample teaching on the practice of the presence of God in his own Carmelite tradition, from the prophet Elijah onwards. Carmelite tradition looks to the Old Testament prophet who founded a school of prophets on Mount Carmel as their spiritual father, and to his cry, 'As the Lord lives, before whom I stand', (e.g. 1 *Kings* 17:1). In many ways, Lawrence was very like Elijah, with his rough exterior, the hard trials he had to endure, and above all the dogged faith and love that brought him through, standing always in the presence of God, to listen to, and hear, his still small voice in the calm after the storm.

As we have seen, in the novitiate Lawrence was introduced to the writings of Teresa of Avila and John of the Cross, and he would have found ample encouragement there to seek the presence of God. Although he might not have found, in his early years, the happiness that Saint John of the Cross revealed, he would have found in this description an accurate assessment of his own later state:

> Oh then, soul, most beautiful among all creatures, so anxious to know the dwelling place of your Beloved that you may go in quest of Him and be united with him, now we are telling you that you yourself are His dwelling and His secret chamber and hiding place. This is something of immense gladness for you, to see that all your good and hope is so close to you as to be within you, or better, that you cannot be without Him.[14]

> What more do you want, O soul! And what else do you search for outside, when within yourself you possess your riches, delights, satisfactions, fullness, and kingdom – your Beloved whom you desire and seek? Be joyful and gladdened in your interior recollection with Him, for you have Him so close to you. Desire Him there, adore Him there.[15]

And in the concise words of Saint Teresa, 'Soul, you must seek yourself in Me, and in yourself seek Me'.

Practising the presence of God

One of the first considerations to recall is that we can seek the presence of God because he is already there. Jesus said, 'Behold, I stand at the door and knock. If anyone opens I will come in and eat with him.'

Our part is to turn the key in the lock and open the door to him. The key may be rusty from disuse and neglect, and it would do no good to force it lest it break. So this practice of the presence of God should not be forced and burdensome, but the key should be oiled by love, which is the motive for seeking God's presence. Lawrence wrote humorously to a Prioress that one of her sisters was 'going ahead of grace'. Rather, he said, it should be taken gently, step by step.

He recognised that not everyone would attain to the perfection of this practice, with some having a greater capacity, others less; nonetheless, this simple and easy way was open to everyone, whatever their calling and state in life.

Lawrence describes the practice of the presence of God as: 'It is to take delight in and become accustomed to his divine company.'[16] In this, we can use our imagination. This is not implying that the presence of God is imaginary, but that we should use this God-given faculty in God's service. Lawrence loved the Gospels above all, and they became almost his only reading; a good way is to imagine a scene from the Gospels and to imagine Jesus present no less now than he was two thousand years ago. We can also use our understanding, or the intellect, which he describes as a general and loving awareness of God, without forming a mental picture of how, for example, Jesus would have looked and talked during his earthly ministry.

Quiet conversation of the soul

Lawrence said that he 'devoted himself to remaining in his holy presence by simple attentiveness and a general loving awareness of God,' that could also be described as a quiet and secret conversation of the soul with God that is lasting.[17]

In this he was undoubtedly guided by Saint Teresa of Avila who said that prayer was nothing other than a loving converse with him whom we know loves us. In this conversation there is no need to search for high-minded phrases. Lawrence was very direct with his Friend; for example, when he failed he simply acknowledged his failure, saying, 'I will never do anything right if you leave me alone; it's up to you to stop me from falling and correct what is wrong'.[18]

The awareness of God's presence could be maintained with a simple phrase; Lawrence gave examples that he himself used, 'My God, I am completely yours' or 'God of love, I love you with all my heart', or 'Lord, fashion me according to your heart';[19] but it could also be without words, just by a simple raising of the heart and mind to God, a loving glance or a movement of the heart.

Distractions must not discourage

Distractions and how to deal with them is a constant theme in any discussion of prayer. Lawrence says that the main thing is that we do not become discouraged:

> Since much time and effort are required to acquire this practice, we must not get discouraged when we fail, for the habit is only formed with effort, yet once it is formed we will find contentment in everything.[20]

He spoke from his own experience and how he persevered lovingly and gently, to use two of his favourite words:

> I regarded him in my heart as my Father, as my God, I adored him there as often as I could, keeping my mind in his holy presence, and recalling him as many times as I was distracted. I had some trouble doing this exercise, but continued in spite of all the difficulties I encountered, without getting disturbed or anxious when I was involuntarily distracted.[21]

As he wrote to a nun who complained about distractions:

> You are telling me nothing new, and you are not the only one who experiences distractions. The mind is extremely flighty... If your mind wanders or withdraws occasionally, don't get upset. Since these disturbances tend to distract the mind rather than focus it, we must use the will to gently collect our thoughts.[22]

One remedy that he had found for himself was that if we get into the habit of thinking of God during the day then distractions during prayer will be less:

> An easy way to keep the mind from wandering during the time of mental prayer, is to keep it as still as possible – not to let it take flight – during the day. You must keep it faithfully in God's presence; and once you are accustomed to think of him from time to time, it will be easy to remain calm during prayer, or at least to bring the mind back when it wanders.[23]

Constant awareness of God's love

Even when we are doing spiritual reading, saying prayers such as the rosary, at Mass, Lawrence says that we can do all these 'holy' things without actually being mindful of God. We can be thinking of God and the things of God, but we also need to take time to stand back, as it were, to remind ourselves to whom we are praying, about whom we are reading, who we are worshipping, and so bring our awareness of God's presence more vividly to mind as we adore and worship him:

> During our work and other activities, even during our reading and writing, no matter how spiritual - and, I emphasise, even during our religious exercises and vocal prayers - we must stop for a moment, as often as possible, to adore God in the depths of our hearts, to savour him, even though in passing and stealthily. Since you are aware that God is present to you during your actions, that he is in the depths and centre of your heart, stop your activities and even your vocal prayers, at least from time to time, to adore him within, to praise him, to ask his help, to offer him your heart, and to thank him.[24]

In this extract Lawrence makes no distinction between what could be called secular and sacred activities. All can be and must be, offered to God because all are part of life, just as Jesus said 'when you pray' not 'if you pray', because prayer is an integral to human living, to being truly human. He took prayer, our seeking the face of his Father, as a natural human activity in life, to be taken for granted. So, Lawrence says, seeking the presence of God within is to adore, to praise, to ask his help, to draw God into every aspect of life. So habitual had this become that he could say that 'By the multiplicity of acts of faith and love, I arrived at a state in which it would have been just as impossible not to think about God as it was difficult to get used to doing so in the beginning.[25]

Living a life of prayer

His long dark night of purification and testing was over, and now Lawrence could write to his spiritual director about his present state, a state that was simplicity itself:

> Since that time I do my work in simple faith before God, humbly and lovingly, and I carefully apply myself to avoid doing, saying, or thinking anything that might displease him. I hope that, having done all I can, he will do with me as he pleases.[26]

A friendly portrait

His great friend, Joseph de Beaufort, painted this portrait of him in this gracious maturity into which he had emerged:

> His attention to spiritual things through prayer makes him gentle, affable, patient and, at the same time, firm in resisting temptation, allowing neither pleasure nor pain to take hold of him. The joy of contemplation, which continually nourishes without ever satisfying him, does not allow him to experience the world's insignificant pleasures. He lives with the Lord by love, even though his body seems to be on earth. He no

longer has any desire for the good things of this world because he has experienced the inaccessible light through faith, and, therefore, love has taken him where he is supposed to be. He desires nothing because he already possesses the objects of his desire to the extent possible in this life.

He has no need of boldness because nothing in this life disturbs him, nor is capable of turning him away from the love of God. He does not need to compose himself because he never yields to sadness, for he is convinced all is well. He never gets angry, nor does anything move him, because he always loves God and is entirely directed to him alone. He is never jealous because he lacks nothing. He loves no one in ordinary friendship, but he loves the Creator through his creatures. His soul is completely constant, free from all change, and now he clings exclusively to God, for he has forgotten all else.[27]

This is a remarkable portrait of someone who has achieved, through the grace of God, an exceptional equilibrium and spiritual maturity, and the consistent testimony is that this portrait is no exaggeration.

From the kitchen to making sandals

His leg was causing him increasing pain, and when, after fifteen years of working in the kitchen, it became ulcerated, Lawrence was transferred to the sandal-making room, where he could sit down more. Even so, he would go to the kitchen on occasion, feast-days perhaps, and when the brothers were especially busy, to help out, peeling the vegetables and other tasks. Lawrence was content with any place, with any task. He found joy everywhere, doing little things for the love of God.

He also had more contact with the world outside the monastery and twice was sent on an assignment to buy wine for the community, the first, a long trip in 1665 to the Auvergne and the year after to Boulogne. This journey was by boat, a very difficult assignment for him with his lame leg, and the only way he could move about the boat was by rolling over the barrels. Although he had no experience of business and felt himself totally unsuited to the task; he told God that was his problem, and he said that without knowing how or why, all was done well.

Loving service

At the monastery he had to deal with the many people, beggars and the poor who came to the door, visitors to the monastery and those who came to pray in the church. Lawrence said that he lived as if there was only God and himself in the world; this might give the impression that he was aloof and unapproachable, but this was very far from the truth. As is the case with true holiness and a true mystic, he was the most approachable of men. People from every walk of life were drawn to him by his simple holiness, his kindness, gentleness and sense of humour. At every opportunity he encouraged everyone to practice the presence of God, and he was often called to the monastery parlour to guide people in their prayer.

Within the monastery, the young friars, seeing Lawrence walking silently through the cloisters and passages, rapt in God, could see in him the living example of a life of prayer that they aspired to live, and increasingly drew on his wisdom. For Lawrence himself, he never tired of encouraging these young men to live life in God to the full. He often regretted that he hadn't served God more in his youth and urged them not to waste their time. Quoting Saint Augustine, 'Goodness ever ancient, ever new, too late have I loved you!' he would add: 'do not waste your time, brothers, you are young. Take advantage of the sincere confession I am making to you of my lack of concern for God's service during my early years. Devote all yours to his love! As for me, if I had known earlier, if someone had told me the things I am now telling you, I would not have delayed in loving him. Believe me, and count as lost all the time not spent in loving God'.[28]

Example of great goodness

It was not only the poor who sought him out, but increasingly, important people began to hear of this holy friar. One of these was Fr. Joseph de Beaufort, counsel and grand vicar to Cardinal de Noailles, the Archbishop of Paris. He asked to see Brother Lawrence, but Lawrence sent back the message that he would agree to meet him only if he wanted to discuss the things of God and not indulge in worldly gossip. Joseph assured him that was also his intent, and on the 3 August 1666, the two men first met. It was a seminal meeting because Joseph became a firm friend over many years. He recorded the conversations they had and Joseph became his first biographer and editor of his writings. It was Joseph who gave a beautiful pen-portrait of Lawrence:

> Brother Lawrence's virtue never made him harsh. His heart was open, eliciting confidence, letting you feel that you could tell him anything and that you had found a friend. For his part, once he knew who he was dealing with, he spoke freely and showed great goodness. What he said was simple, yet always appropriate, and made good sense. Once you got past his rough exterior you discovered an unusual wisdom, a freedom beyond the reach of the ordinary lay brother, an insight that extended far beyond what you would expect. When he was seeking alms you could see he was suited to conduct the most serious business, and you could consult him on anything. Such was the appearance Brother Lawrence gave.[29]

Avoiding the limelight

He added another description in his Eulogy after Brother Lawrence's death; after his breakthrough into serenity, Joseph said:

> He seemed to be naturally disposed to virtue, gentle in mood, completely righteous, with the best heart in the world. His fine countenance, his human, affable air, his simple, modest manner won him the esteem and good will of all who saw him. The more closely you looked, the more you discovered in him a depth of integrity and piety rarely found elsewhere. People noticed that one of his concerns was not to let any singularity show in his actions. He always followed the simplicity of the common life without putting on the austere, melancholy air that only serves to discourage people. He was not one of those inflexible people who consider sanctity incompatible with ordinary manners. He associated with everyone and never put on airs, acting kindly toward his brothers and friends without wanting to be conspicuous.[30]

De Beaufort said that Lawrence did not want to be conspicuous, but sometimes this was difficult; in his first extant letter he admits to a nun that sometimes the burning love of God within him was so intense that he had to resort to acting foolishly to disguise his ecstasy, a behaviour, he said, that made him look more foolish than holy.[31]

The quietist controversy

Brother Lawrence became increasingly ill with his ulcerated leg and three times was near death. His patience and contentment in sickness was just as it was as when he was in comparative health, for the thought of death held no terrors for him. When the doctor managed to bring down his fever during one of these crises Lawrence remarked, 'Ah, doctor, your remedies have worked too well for me; you only delay my happiness!'[32]

Growing reputation and writings

During these years of increasing infirmity he had more time to write and to put down his thoughts, his Spiritual Maxims, on the spiritual life. He did not find it easy to put down in words what he experienced and threw away many a sheet of paper.

Most of his extant letters were written during these latter years. Unfortunately, Beaufort removed the names of the recipients of the letters when he published them after Lawrence's death, so we know only vague details of who they were. One of them was a Blessed Sacrament nun who had a convent next to the Carmelites, and another was a Carmelite nun, perhaps the Prioress of the Paris community.

He was also becoming increasingly known and admired outside of the monastery and attracted eminent visitors. One of these visitors was Archbishop de Noailles, the Archbishop of Paris. At his recommendation, Fénelon, his friend and vicar general, also visited Lawrence during his last illness. François Fénelon was one of the most famous orators in France, tutor to the Dauphin, and Bishop of Cambrai, and wrote later of the encounter:

> The words of the saints themselves are often very different from the discourse of those who tried to describe them. Saint Catherine of Genoa was prodigious in love. Brother Lawrence of the Resurrection was rough in nature but delicate in grace. This mixture was appealing, and revealed God present in him. I saw him, and there is a place in the book where the author, without mentioning me by name, briefly related a fine conversation I had with him on death, and even though he was very sick, he remained very happy.[33]

Fénelon had asked him if he would be willing to live on for many more years, despite his suffering. Lawrence replied simply that he was totally surrendered to the will of God and what he wanted. This meeting with Lawrence was also important for the influence it had on Fénélon and the Quietist controversy in which he was to become embroiled.

Quietism summarised

At this time quietism was causing a great deal of controversy. This was a form of prayer and spirituality that drew a great deal on Eastern mysticism and a Gnostic belief that anything material was evil, and that in prayer one had to hold oneself totally passively and allow God to do everything. It was the Spaniard, Michael de Molinos, earlier in the 17th Century, who expounded quietism in its most extreme form, and which was condemned by the Church. The main propositions condemned were:

It is necessary that [man] reduce [his] powers to nothingness and in this consists the interior way.

The will to work actively is an offence to God, who wishes to be Himself the sole agent; and, therefore, one must totally abandon one's whole self in God and thereafter remain like a lifeless body.

Natural activity is the enemy of grace and it hinders God's action and true perfection, because God wishes to act in us without us.

By doing nothing the soul annihilates itself and returns to its principle and origin, which is the essence of God, in which it remains transformed and divinised....

For one who is resigned to the divine will it is not proper to ask anything from God; because asking is an imperfection, since it is an act of one's own will and choice. And it is to wish that the divine will be conformed to our own, and not our own to the divine will; and the passage of the Gospel saying, 'Ask and you will receive' (*John* 16:24) was not said by Christ for interior souls who refuse to have a will; moreover, these kinds of souls reach the point when they cannot ask anything from God.[34]

Madame Guyon's role

At this time the most famous and influential advocate of quietism was Madame Jeanne Guyon. Born 13 April 1648, she married Jacques Guyon, 22 years older than herself, when she was 16. She bore him five children, two of whom died. After twelve years of an unhappy marriage Jacques also died, leaving her with her three remaining children. Jeanne had at one point wanted to become a nun, and now, as a widow, she devoted herself to the spiritual life, publishing several books, bearing striking similarities to Molinos' quietism. Her first two books were published in the 1680s and in 1688 were placed on the *Index*, the list of forbidden books because of the quietist errors they contained.

However, she had a champion in Fénélon, who first met her in 1688 and who became a firm supporter of her undoubted piety, and her spiritual teaching, which could more properly be called semi-quietism, because it did not go as far as Molinos' propositions. Jeanne Guyon herself admitted her mistakes to a commission set up to investigate her writings, although she never amended them in her books.

Genuine abandonment versus errors in quietism

After his death, Brother Lawrence was dragged into the quietist controversy because Fénélon engaged in a heated debate with Jacques Bossuet[35] over one particular aspect of quietism. Fénélon believed that there was a state of Pure Love attainable in this life in which the soul was no longer concerned with its own salvation, with thoughts of heaven and hell, of reward or punishment. In support he quoted the words of Brother Lawrence, that 'since I entered religious life I no longer think about virtue or my salvation'.

There are such passages in Lawrence's writings which could be read as supporting quietism, but in fact are very far from it. In saying this, Lawrence was not expressing a lack of concern about his salvation, but a total abandonment to the love of God and confidence in God's grace. Giving an account of his soul to his spiritual director he wrote.

I cannot express to you what is taking place in me at present. I feel neither concern nor doubt about my state since I have no will other than the will of God, which I try to carry out in all things and to which I am so surrendered that I would not so much as pick up a straw from the ground against his order, nor for any other reason than pure love.[36]

This, of course, is the exact opposite of quietism. Far from condemning activity, as the quietists did, Lawrence did everything for the love of God. His will was not passive but he actively sought to unite his will with the will of God.

Lawrence said that he sometimes thought of himself as 'a piece of stone before the sculptor who desires to carve a statue; presenting myself in this way before God I ask him to fashion his perfect image in my soul, making me entirely like himself.'[37] This was not a state he sought, as did the quietists, but a state to which he was sometimes raised by the action of God's grace. For Lawrence, this was not a passive thing, because he held himself actively before God, he was 'presenting himself', co-operating totally with the divine action within.

He went on to say that 'At other times, as soon as I apply myself I feel my whole mind and soul raised without trouble or effort, and it remains suspended and permanently rooted in God as in its centre and place of rest'. Brother Lawrence attained to this rest in God in the centre of his being by co-operating with the grace of God, not remaining inert and passive.

Lawrence answered a possible charge that his state could be seen as quietism by continuing:

> I know that some would call this state idleness, self-deception and self-love. I maintain that it is a holy idleness and a blessed self love, should the soul in this state be capable of it. In fact, when the soul is in this state of rest its former acts (using aids to prayer) do not trouble it; these acts were formerly its support but now they would do more harm than good.

In this he was following Saint John of the Cross, who agreed that external prayers, acts of devotion, and religious pictures, for example, could be used as aids to prayer, but when God himself took over the prayer, as it were, then these aids become superfluous.

> In contemplation the activity of the senses and of discursive reflection terminates, and God alone is the agent and the one Who then speaks secretly to the solitary and silent soul.... Once an individual, through

the activity of his faculties, has reached the quiet recollection which every spiritual person pursues, in which the functioning of these faculties ceases, it would not merely be useless to repeat the acts of these same faculties in order to attain to this recollection, but it would be harmful for, in abandoning the recollection it already possesses, he would become distracted.[38]

In the same way, Lawrence said that he gave up all devotions and prayers that were not required and devoted himself exclusively to remaining always in his holy presence. They had performed their function of placing him in God's presence, but he never denied their usefulness.

Catholic understanding

It has always been the position of Catholic spiritual tradition that, as we are human beings, with body and soul, then external aids are useful until God himself draws the soul into a deeper prayer, and even then there will be occasions when we may still need them. But to deny them altogether is to deny our humanness and the goodness of God's creation. It is only when they become means in themselves that they can draw us away from God.

Likewise, Lawrence never denied the goodness and beauty of the external world and all the helps that are provided to aid us in prayer. As his experience of recognising the renewing love of God in the bare tree of winter had affirmed to him, he saw the goodness of God in everything, and everything in God. He gave himself to God, body and soul:

'It is only right that the heart, the first to beat with life and that controls the rest of the body, should be the first and the last to love and adore God, whether by beginning or by completing our spiritual and physical activities, and generally, in all life's exercises.[39]

Final sufferings

Eventually, Lawrence was too ill to carry on. His last letters speak much of suffering and how to approach it. To a Carmelite nun he wrote:

> I will not ask God to deliver you from your trials but I will ask him earnestly to give you the patience and strength needed to suffer for as long as he desires. Find consolation in him who keeps you fixed to the cross; he will release you when he judges it appropriate. Happy are they who suffer with him. Get used to suffering, and ask him for strength to suffer as he wants, and for as long as he judges necessary. The worldly do not understand these truths, and I am not surprised; the reason is that they suffer as citizens of this world and not as Christians. They consider illnesses as natural afflictions and not as graces from God, and therefore they find in them only what is difficult and harsh for nature. But those who regard them as coming from the hand of God, as signs of his mercy and the means he uses for their salvation, ordinarily find great sweetness and perceptible consolations in them.[40]

Patience and strength from above

This letter sets out very clearly what Lawrence had learnt and applied in his own experience over many decades of increasing suffering. He saw his disability and pain from a supernatural point of view, as something permitted by God for his salvation and to unite him with his Saviour and his saving death. Like Paul, he was making up in his own body what 'is lacking in Christ's afflictions for the sake of his body, that is, the Church'.[41] In his intimate conversations with Christ present to him and in him, Lawrence continually asked him to give him the patience and strength he needed in his suffering. He was truly happy to suffer with Jesus. As he also wrote,

> No matter how great the pain is, accept it with love, for suffering is a paradise as long as we are with him. If we want to enjoy the peace of paradise in this life, we must become accustomed to conversing with him in a familiar, humble and loving manner.[42]

Joseph de Beaufort, who visited him during his final illness, testified that what he wrote and what he encouraged others to do, he himself provided an outstanding example: 'I can testify that he gave signs of altogether extraordinary constancy, resignation and joy during the third illness.' This joy evidently surpassed his suffering, and the brothers testified that it showed not only in his face but in his speaking.

The faith by which he had lived for so many years also seemed paper thin, as if he already tasted heaven: 'what consoles me in this life is that I see God by faith. I see him in such a way that I can sometimes say, "I no longer believe, I see, for I experience what faith teaches." With this assurance, and by this practice of faith, I will live and die with him.'[43]

Desire for suffering and love

The brother who was looking after him wanted to offer him some consolation, but Lawrence replied, 'Thank you, Brother, but please let me suffer a little for the love of God.', and he often prayed, 'My God, I adore you in my sufferings! This is how I will suffer something for you. May I soon suffer and die with you!'

Even though he had enough pain to endure, he even added to it by deliberately turning on his side, where he had pain from pleurisy, to satisfy his ardent desire to suffer. It was only the quick reaction of the brother who saw he would die, being unable to breathe and being in such pain, turned him on his other side and saved his life at that point.

When he heard one of his friends saying 'This is for you, Brother Lawrence. It is time to depart', of the poor bed that had been prepared for him, he replied, 'Yes, it is true. This is my deathbed, but someone who does not expect it at all will follow me immediately.' It was prophetic, because Brother Philibert of the Angels, who was in perfect health, was suddenly taken ill and died the day following Lawrence's own death. It could be that the two were related, because Philibert had the same surname as Lawrence's uncle. They were buried in the same grave.

Prepared for death

For several months Lawrence had told his brothers that he would die before the end of February, and on the 6 February, only a few days before his death, he wrote to the Blessed Sacrament sister that he would soon die, saying, 'Goodbye. I hope to see him soon.'

It was the most intense love of God that sustained him. A friar asked him what he was doing, and Lawrence replied, 'I am doing what I will be doing for all eternity; I am blessing God, I am praising God, I am adoring him, and I am loving him with my whole heart. Our whole vocation consists of this, brothers, to love and adore God without worrying about anything else.[44]

The next day, Monday, 12 February, 1691, at nine o'clock in the morning, fully conscious, without agony or convulsions, Brother Lawrence of the Resurrection died in the embrace of the Lord and offered his soul to God with the peace and tranquillity of one asleep.[45]

Perhaps the best testimony with which we can conclude is to repeat what Fénélon wrote in a letter of 5 August 1700:

> You have seen many saints that love instructed without learning, for no trace of a human hand was to be found there. It is not astonishing that love teaches us to love. Those who love sincerely, and whom the Spirit of God inebriates with his new wine, speak an entirely new language. When you feel what others do not feel, and what you yourself have not felt before, you express this the best way you can, and almost always find that the expression only partly conveys the reality.[46]

Maxims of Brother Lawrence of the Resurrection

The holiest, most ordinary, and most necessary practice in the spiritual life is that of the presence of God. It consists in taking delight in and becoming accustomed to his divine company, speaking humbly and conversing lovingly with him all the time, at every moment, without rule or measure; especially in times of temptation, suffering, aridity, weariness, even infidelity and sin.[47]

There is no way of life in the world more agreeable or delightful than continual conversation with God; only those who practice and experience it can understand this…We must not seek consolations from this exercise, but must do it from a motive of love, and because God wants it.[48]

Adoring God in spirit and in truth means adoring God as we are supposed to adore him. God is spirit and we must adore him in spirit and in truth, that is, with humble and authentic adoration of spirit in the depths and centre of our souls. God alone can see this adoration, which we can repeat so often that in the end it will become second nature to us, as if God were one with our souls and our souls were one with God.[49]

I say that this gentle, loving awareness of God imperceptibly ignites a divine fire in the soul, inflaming it so intensely with love of God that one is forced to perform various activities in an effort to contain it.[50]

We must cultivate faith, hope and love, and for these alone can conform us completely to the will of God. All other things are insignificant and we must not settle for them, but rather regard them as a bridge to be crossed quickly so we can lose ourselves in our sole end by confidence and love.[51]

We must keep our eyes fixed on God in everything we say, do or undertake. Our goal is to be the most perfect adorers of God in this life as we hope to be through all eternity.[52]

A brief lifting up of the heart is enough. A brief remembrance of God, an act of adoration – even though on the run with sword in hand – these prayers, short as they may be, are pleasing to God and, far from causing those engaged in battle to lose courage in the most dangerous of circumstances, fortify them.[53]

It is impossible to avoid the dangers and hazards which life is full of without God's actual, constant help; let us ask him for it continually. We cannot ask him for it unless we are with him. we cannot be with him unless we think of him often. We cannot think of him often unless we habitually practice this holy exercise.[54]

Gradually become accustomed to adoring him in this way, asking him for his grace, offering him your heart from time to time, during the day, while at work, at every possible moment. Do not force yourself to follow special rules or practice private devotions; do this in faith, with love and humility.[55]

I regarded him in my heart as my Father and my God. I adored him there as often as I could, keeping my mind in his holy presence, and recalling him as many times as I was distracted. I had some trouble doing this exercise, but continued in spite of all the difficulties I encountered, without getting disturbed or anxious when I was involuntarily distracted. I was as faithful to this practice during my activities as I was during my periods of mental prayer, for every moment, all the time, in the most intense periods of my work I banished and rid from my mind everything that was capable of taking the thought of God away from me.[56]

Endnotes

1 Cf. 1 Cor. 1:18-28
2 Light of the World p.17
3 Letter 7 p. 63ff
4 Ways 6 p.114ff
5 Eulogy 15 p.8
6 The Principles 8 p.36
7 Eulogy 49 p.10
8 Letter 2 p. 53
9 Eulogy 22 p.10
10 Eulogy 28 p.11
11 Ways 12 p.92
12 Letter 2 p.53
13 Letter 15 p.81
14 Spiritual Canticle Stanza 1:7
15 *Ibid* Stanza 1:8
16 Spiritual Maxims 7 p.36
17 Letter 2 p. 53
18 Conversations 16 p.92
19 Spiritual Maxims 30 p.41
20 *Ibid* 29 p.41
21 Letter 12 p.75
22 Letter 7 p.65
23 *Ibid*
24 Spiritual Maxims 9 p.36ff
25 Eulogy 30 p.12
26 Letter 2 p.53
27 Ways 30,31 p.122ff
28 Eulogy 48 p.19
29 Ways p.113ff
30 Eulogy 35 p.14

31 In his letters and writings Brother Lawrence, in his humility, sometimes referred to himself in the third person.
32 Eulogy 51 p.20
33 Introduction p.xxi
34 Neuner SJ & Dupuis SJ, eds: The Christian Faith, Collins p.587ff
35 Bossuet, Bishop of Meaux, was one of the greatest orators of his age and also at one point tutor to the Grand Dauphin.
36 Letter 2 p.53
37 Letter 2 p.54
38 Saint John of the Cross, The Living Flame of Love 3:44,45
39 Spiritual Maxims 29 p.41
40 Letter 11 p.73
41 Colossians 1:24
42 Letter 15 p. 81
43 Letter 11 p.74
44 Eulogy 59 p.23
45 Eulogy 60 p.23
46 P.191
47 Spiritual Maxims 6
48 Letter 3
49 Spiritual Maxims 12
50 Spiritual Maxims 24
51 4th Conversation
52 Spiritual Maxims 2
53 Letter 6
54 Letter 8
55 Letter 9
56 Letter 12

All references to Brother Lawrence come from: *The Practice of the Presence of God*. Trans. Salvatore Sciurba, OCD. ICS, 1994

Benedict XVI
THE FATHERS & WRITERS OF
THE FIRST MILLENNIUM
The Spiritual Masters

The ten catecheses in this richly illustrated volume take us back to the historical period immediately following the first Fathers of the Church. Each of the Spiritual Masters described by Pope Benedict left their own mark on the Church's culture and spirituality and helped in her growth.

ISBN: 978 1 86082 772-8
CTS Code: B 739

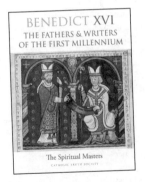

Benedict XVI
THE MEDIEVAL FATHERS & WRITERS
The Spiritual Masters

Through his series of catecheses on the life and works of great witnesses to the faith, Pope Benedict XVI helps us to understand "what it means to be a Christian today." These portraits of the distinguished figures of the medieval Church are not just biographical sketches but also provide the ecclesial backdrop against which they lived out their 'yes' to Christ. Through the words of the Holy Father, these great Saints and teachers of the faith come alive and call us to reawaken and deepen our own faith.

ISBN: 978 1 86082 723 5
CTS Code: B 740

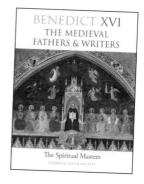

BENEDICT XVI
THE MEDIEVAL
FATHERS & WRITERS

The Spiritual Masters
CATHOLIC TRUTH SOCIETY

A world of Catholic reading at your fingertips...

Catholic Faith, Life & Truth for all

www.cts-online.org.uk

CTS CATHOLIC COMPASS

ctscatholiccompass.org

twitter: @CTSpublishers

facebook.com/CTSpublishers

Catholic Truth Society, Publishers to the Holy See.